ALL RIGHTS RESERVED

To book the Author for a book review, media appearance &/or speaking engagements, please send a request to:
info@jaforafox.com

ISBN: 979-8-218-26328-7

Published By: Author Overnight Publications & Designs
www.authorovernight.info

This Book Belongs To:

INTRODUCTION

Welcome to the Free To Love Me Devotional Journal, a transformative guide designed to accompany you on a profound journey of healing, self-discovery, and spiritual growth.

Embrace the power of self-love, faith, and personal transformation as you embark on this empowering expedition.

Allow the truth of God's Word to shape your thoughts, words, and beliefs, guiding you on a journey towards embracing your identity, experiencing healing, and walking in the freedom to love yourself unconditionally.

Embrace the transformative power of God's love and live a life filled with self-acceptance, joy, and purpose as you discover the freedom to love yourself and others with an open heart.

WELCOME!

I am writing to express my gratitude for your recent purchase of the Free To Love Me Devotional Journal. Your support means the world to me, and I am genuinely thankful for your decision to invest in my work.

Creating this devotional journal has been a labor of love, and I am thrilled that it has found its way into your hands. This journal will be a source of inspiration, self-reflection, and spiritual growth on your journey. I sincerely desire that it brings you closer to experiencing the freedom, love, and fulfillment of embracing your identity in Christ.

Your purchase supports me as a creator and encourages me to continue sharing my passion for spreading God's love and truth. Knowing that my work has resonated with you brings me great joy and reaffirms the purpose behind what I do.

Once again, thank you for choosing the Free To Love Me Devotional Journal. Your support is invaluable. If you have any questions or feedback, please don't hesitate to reach out. I would be delighted to hear about your experience with the journal.

May God's blessings overflow in your life as you embark on this journey of self-discovery and spiritual growth.

With heartfelt appreciation,

Jafora Fox

DEDICATION

Thank you to my husband, Deacon Derrick Fox, and my Sons, Darron Wright, Jr. & Ja'Ron Wright, for your Love and Support.

In loving memory of my Parents; Jaford Dove, Sr. & Mary Frances Dove #LoveDove

Pray More, Talk Less
Matthew 6:7 (AMP)

"And when you pray, do not use meaningless repetition as the Gentiles do, for they think they will be heard because of their many words."

When you Pray about it, don't keep talking about it! Prayer changes things, but you must allow God the time to come in and change things! Give it to Him in prayer.

Declare: Something Great is going to happen for me today. Walk in Expectation.

Action: Do you have a situation you need to pray about?

_____

_____

_____

_____

_____

_____

_____

_____

_____

_____

_____

_____

_____

_____

_____

_____

_____

_____

Reflect

Things on my heart:

_____
_____
_____
_____
_____
_____

Things I'm grateful for:

_____
_____
_____
_____
_____
_____

Prayer Requests:

_____
_____
_____
_____
_____
_____

 Declaration:

I am free to love me!

DATE:

Things on my heart...

Walking In

Victory

Wisdom

Proverbs 2:6 (AMP)

"For the Lord gives [skillful and godly] wisdom; From His mouth come knowledge and understanding."

My prayer for today is that the Lord opens the eyes of your understanding and blesses you with wisdom!

Declare: Something Great is going to happen for me today.
Walk in Expectation.

<u>Action: What area in your life do you need wisdom and understanding?</u>

_____

_____

_____

_____

_____

_____

_____

_____

_____

_____

_____

_____

_____

_____

_____

_____

_____

_____

_____

Reflect

Things on my heart:

_____
_____
_____
_____
_____
_____

Things I'm grateful for:

_____
_____
_____
_____
_____

Prayer Requests:

_____
_____
_____
_____
_____

 Declaration:

I am free to love me!

Things on my heart...

I am free to love me
Word Search

G	W	I	L	O	V	E	P	L	E	G
R	S	E	L	F	C	A	R	E	P	O
W	B	O	S	S	B	F	R	E	E	A
T	R	I	E	F	I	T	V	C	C	L
E	E	U	N	I	C	O	N	A	E	F
F	R	E	S	I	L	I	E	N	T	T
U	A	T	N	T	Y	P	R	N	D	K
L	E	O	B	E	Y	O	U	D	L	D
S	B	E	A	U	T	I	F	U	L	O
T	B	E	L	O	N	G	S	E	L	G
B	E	L	I	E	V	E	M	O	C	C

GOD   LOVE   BEAUTIFUL

SELF CARE   GOALS   BELONG

RESILIENT   GRATEFUL   FREE

PEACE   BE YOU   BELIEVE

Favor
Proverbs 3:4 (AMP)

"So find favor and high esteem In
the sight of God and man."

I decree and declare that you shall walk in favor! Everywhere your feet shall strode is blessed! Great doors of opportunity shall open for you! Continue to Keep the Faith. Don't give up. You have come too far to turn back now. Keep your eyes on God. Watch God show up and show out on your behalf.

Declare: Something Great is going to happen for me today. Walk in Expectation.

Action: In what area in your life do you need the favor of God?

_____

_____

_____

_____

_____

_____

_____

_____

_____

_____

_____

_____

_____

_____

_____

_____

_____

_____

_____

Reflect

Things on my heart:

_____
_____
_____
_____
_____
_____

Things I'm grateful for:

_____
_____
_____
_____
_____
_____

Prayer Requests:

_____
_____
_____
_____
_____
_____

 **Declaration:**

I am free to love me!

Things on my heart...

The Prayer Of Jabez
1 Chronicles 4:10 (AMP)

"Jabez (your name) cried out to the God of Israel, saying, "Oh that You would indeed bless me (your name) and enlarge my border [property], and that Your hand would be with me (your name), and You would keep me from evil so that it does not hurt me (your name)!" And God granted his (your name) request."

free
TO LOVE ME

My prayer is that God will Bless you and Enlarge your territory!
Hang in there! God is going to grant your request!

Declare: Something Great is going to happen for me today.
Walk in Expectation.

Action: Write your Jabez prayer below.

_____

_____

_____

_____

_____

_____

_____

_____

_____

_____

_____

_____

_____

_____

_____

_____

_____

_____

_____

Reflect

Things on my heart:

_____
_____
_____
_____
_____
_____

Things I'm grateful for:

_____
_____
_____
_____
_____
_____

Prayer Requests:

_____
_____
_____
_____
_____
_____

Declaration:

I am free to love me!

Things on my heart...

_____

_____

_____

_____

_____

_____

_____

_____

_____

_____

_____

_____

_____

_____

_____

_____

_____

_____

_____

_____

_____

_____

_____

Prayer Works
John 14:27 (AMP)

"Peace I leave with you; My [perfect] peace I give to you; not as the world gives do I give to you. Do not let your heart be troubled, nor let it be afraid. [Let My perfect peace calm you in every circumstance and give you courage and strength for every challenge.]"

free
TO LOVE ME

Do not be troubled or afraid. God is in Control. I speak Peace in your heart, mind, home, thoughts, situations, workplace, and every area of your life.

**Declare: Something Great is going to happen for me today.
Walk in Expectation.**

<u>Action: What areas in your life do you need Peace?</u>

_____

_____

_____

_____

_____

_____

_____

_____

_____

_____

_____

_____

_____

_____

_____

_____

_____

Reflect

Things on my heart:

_____
_____
_____
_____
_____
_____

Things I'm grateful for:

_____
_____
_____
_____
_____
_____

Prayer Requests:

_____
_____
_____
_____
_____
_____

 Declaration:

I am free to love me!

Things on my heart...

God Answers Prayers
Mark 11:24 (AMP)

"For this reason I am telling you, whatever things you ask for in prayer [in accordance with God's will], believe [with confident trust] that you have received them, and they will be given to you."

free
TO LOVE ME

We serve a Prayer answering God! Keep Praying! Keep Believing!

Declare: Something Great is going to happen for me today.
Walk in Expectation.

Action: Write your prayer request below.

_____

_____

_____

_____

_____

_____

_____

_____

_____

_____

_____

_____

_____

_____

_____

_____

_____

_____

 *Reflect*

Things on my heart:

_____
_____
_____
_____
_____
_____

Things I'm grateful for:

_____
_____
_____
_____
_____
_____

Prayer Requests:

_____
_____
_____
_____
_____
_____

 *Declaration:*

I am free to love me!

Things on my heart...

Good Plans
Jeremiah 29:11 (NIV)

"For I know the plans I have for you (your name)," declares the Lord, "plans to prosper you (your name) and not to harm you (your name), plans to give you (your name) hope and a future."

free
TO LOVE ME

Life can sometimes bring you to a place where you're not sure of the plans for your life. Uncertainty can bring emotions such as anxiety, fear, worry, and doubt. When you find your thoughts emotional, apply the word of God.

Declare: Something Great is going to happen for me today. Walk in Expectation.

<u>Action: Write Jeremiah 29:11 and put your name.</u>

_____

_____

_____

_____

_____

_____

_____

_____

_____

_____

_____

_____

_____

_____

_____

_____

_____

_____

Reflect

Things on my heart:

_____

_____

_____

_____

_____

_____

Things I'm grateful for:

_____

_____

_____

_____

_____

Prayer Requests:

_____

_____

_____

_____

_____

 **Declaration:**

I am free to love me!

Self-love Crossword Puzzle

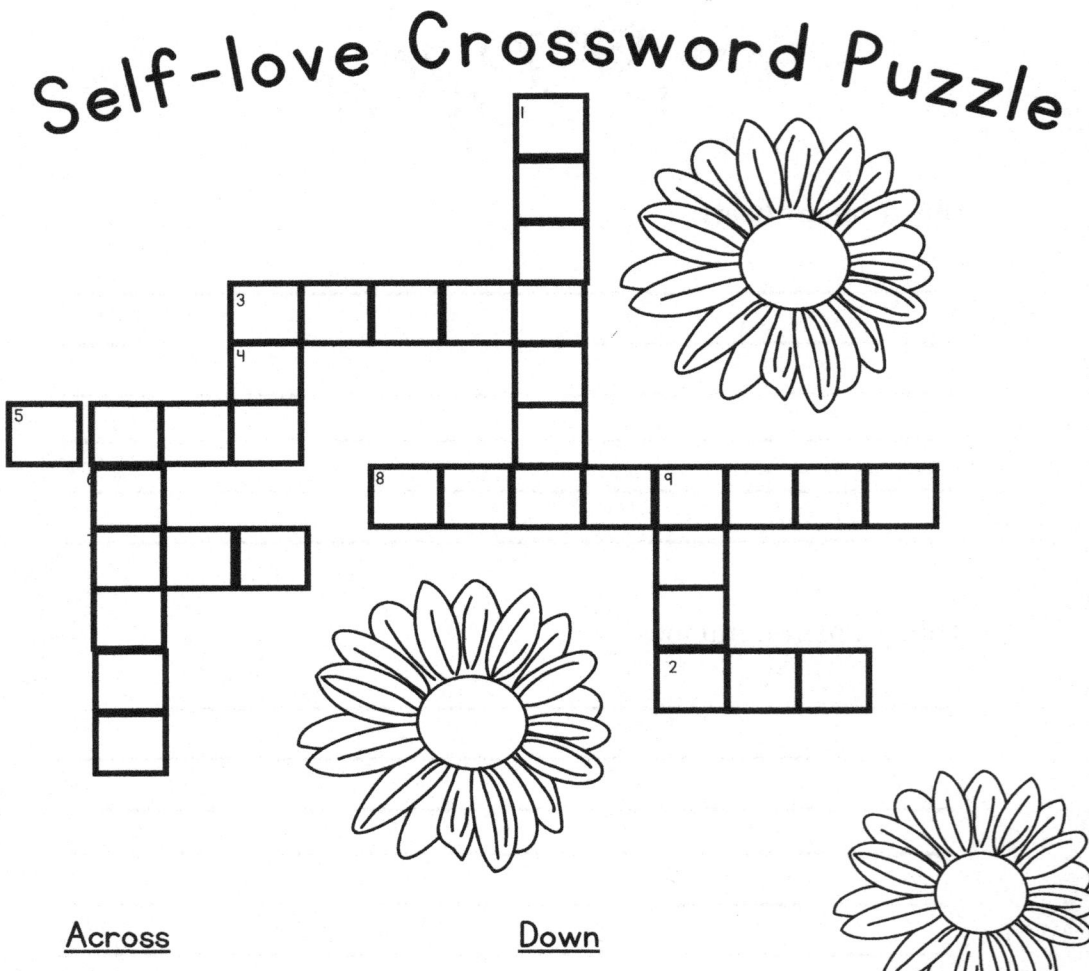

Across

2. Have an ___ to hear

4. When you give your life to God youi become _____

5. Taking care of your ____ is important to aging with confidence

7. When relationships or environments no longer serve you, they must some to an ___.

8. regard for one's own well-being and happiness is _____

Down

1. the quality or state of being

3. Disobedience is a ___

6. _____that surpasses all understanding

9. To have deep feelings of affection for yourself or others

Self-love Crossword Puzzle

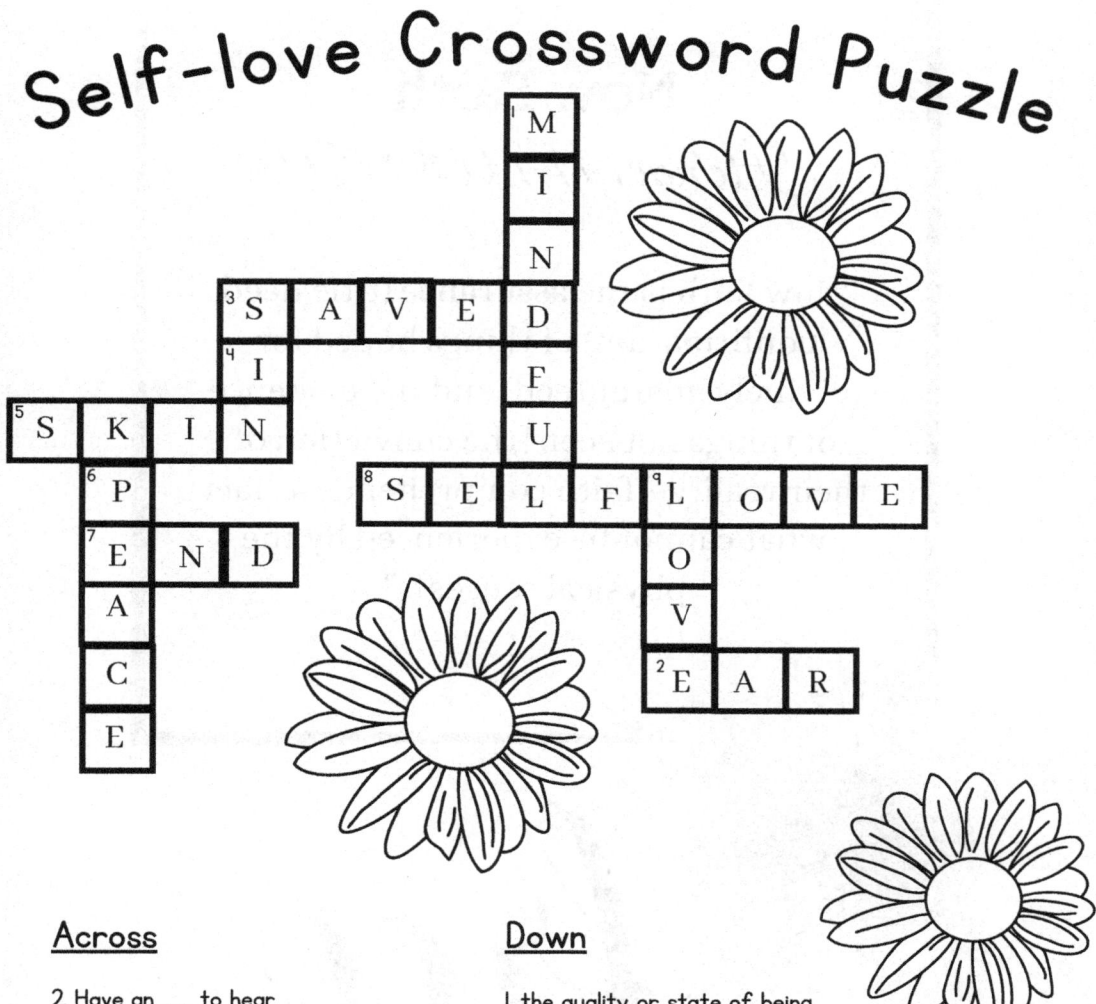

Across

2. Have an ___ to hear

4. When you give your life to God youi become _____

5. Taking care of your ____ is important to aging with confidence

7. When relationships or environments no longer serve you, they must some to an ___.

8. regard for one's own well-being and happiness is _____

Down

1. the quality or state of being

3. Disobedience is a ___

6. _____that surpasses all understanding

9. To have deep feelings of affection for yourself or others

Now Faith

Hebrews 11:1 (AMP)

"Now faith is the assurance (title deed, confirmation) of things hoped for (divinely guaranteed) and the evidence of things not seen [the conviction of their reality—faith comprehends as fact what cannot be experienced by the physical senses].."

free
TO LOVE ME

Keep a NOW Faith, no matter what it looks or feels like. God is working everything out for your good.

**Declare: Something Great is going to happen for me today.
Walk in Expectation.**

<u>Action: What areas in your life do you need God to move on NOW?</u>

_____

_____

_____

_____

_____

_____

_____

_____

_____

_____

_____

_____

_____

_____

_____

_____

_____

Things on my heart:

_____

_____

_____

_____

_____

_____

Things I'm grateful for:

_____

_____

_____

_____

_____

_____

Prayer Requests:

_____

_____

_____

_____

_____

_____

I am free to love me!

Things on my heart...

God Is Not The Author of Confusion

1 Corinthians 14:33 (AMP)

"for God [who is the source of their prophesying] is not a God of confusion and disorder but of peace and order. As [is the practice] in all the churches of the saints (God's people)."

free
TO LOVE ME

I speak Peace over Every area of your life.

**Declare: Something Great is going to happen for me today.
Walk in Expectation.**

Action: Ask God to bring peace to a confusing situation.

_____
_____
_____
_____
_____
_____
_____
_____
_____
_____
_____
_____
_____
_____
_____
_____
_____
_____
_____
_____

Reflect

Things on my heart:

_____
_____
_____
_____
_____
_____

Things I'm grateful for:

_____
_____
_____
_____
_____

Prayer Requests:

_____
_____
_____
_____
_____

 **Declaration:**

I am free to love me!

Things on my heart...

Restorer
Deuteronomy 30:3 (AMP)

"then the Lord your God will restore your fortunes [in your return from exile] and have compassion on you, and will gather you together again from all the peoples (nations) where He has scattered you."

free
TO LOVE ME

I speak Restoration over every area of your life.
God will restore your Joy, Peace, Mind, Body, Love, Finance, and Soul.

Declare: Something Great is going to happen for me today.
Walk in Expectation.

Action: What areas of your life do you need Restoration?

_____

_____

_____

_____

_____

_____

_____

_____

_____

_____

_____

_____

_____

_____

_____

_____

_____

Reflect

Things on my heart:

_____

_____

_____

_____

_____

_____

Things I'm grateful for:

_____

_____

_____

_____

_____

_____

Prayer Requests:

_____

_____

_____

_____

_____

_____

 **Declaration:**

I am free to love me!

Things on my heart...

_____

_____

_____

_____

_____

_____

_____

_____

_____

_____

_____

_____

_____

_____

_____

_____

_____

_____

_____

_____

Forgiveness
Mark 11:25 (AMP)

"And when ye stand praying, forgive, if ye have ought against any: that your Father also which is in heaven may forgive you your trespasses."

free
TO LOVE ME

Don't continue to hold onto the pain or hurt of what someone did to you. Embrace forgiveness and move forward! Yes, Even if the other person does not apologize or take responsibility for their actions, you must forgive them. You can forgive the person without excusing the act. Forgiveness brings a kind of peace that helps you go on with life. So, today Forgive and Free Yourself.

Declare: Something Great is going to happen for me today. Walk in Expectation.

<u>Action: Who do you need to forgive?</u>

_____

_____

_____

_____

_____

_____

_____

_____

_____

_____

_____

_____

_____

_____

_____

_____

_____

_____

_____

Reflect

Things on my heart:

_____

_____

_____

_____

_____

_____

Things I'm grateful for:

_____

_____

_____

_____

_____

Prayer Requests:

_____

_____

_____

_____

_____

 **Declaration:**

I am free to love me!

DATE:

Things on my heart...

_____

_____

_____

_____

_____

_____

_____

_____

_____

_____

_____

_____

_____

_____

_____

_____

_____

_____

_____

_____

_____

_____

_____

_____

My Help
Psalms 121:2 (AMP)

"My help cometh from the LORD,
which made heaven and earth."

free
TO LOVE ME

Know that God has not forgotten about You, no matter what it looks, feels, or whatever you need. God cares about every detail of your life.

Declare: Something Great is going to happen for me today.
Walk in Expectation.

Action: What prayers have you forgotten about?
Submit them before the Lord again.

_____

_____

_____

_____

_____

_____

_____

_____

_____

_____

_____

_____

_____

_____

_____

_____

_____

Reflect

Things on my heart:

_____

_____

_____

_____

_____

_____

Things I'm grateful for:

_____

_____

_____

_____

_____

Prayer Requests:

_____

_____

_____

_____

_____

 **Declaration:**

I am free to love me!

DATE:

Things on my heart...

WHEEL OF
LIFE

The wheel of life is a great tool that helps you better understand what you can do to make your life more balanced. Think about the 8 life categories below and color in where you are on the scale.

1-meaning doing really bad at this
10-means I've accomplishedthis.

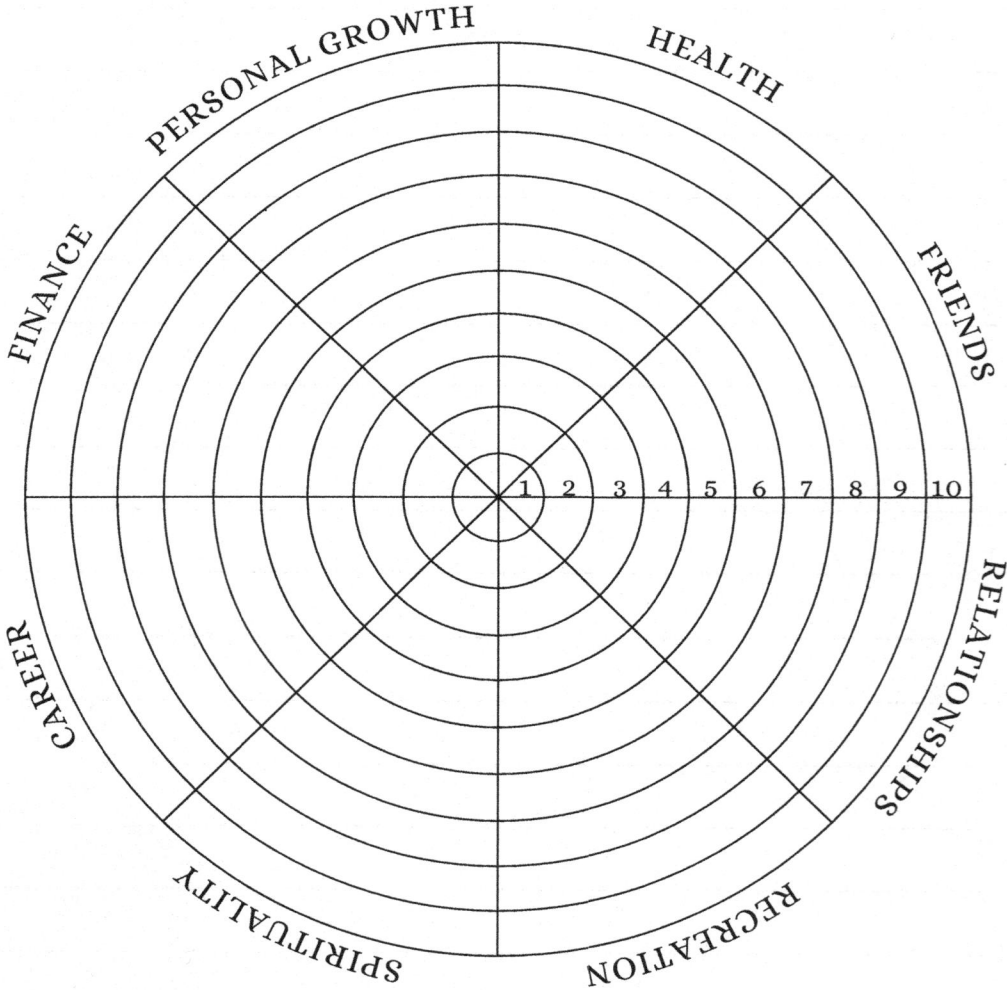

Free
John 8:32 (KJV)

"And ye shall know the truth, and the
truth shall make you free."

If you're in pain, disappointed, tired, sick, frustrated, angry, not feeling well, not having a good day. It's okay. Acknowledge the place you're at but do not stay in that place or continue to revisit it. Deal with your issues, make the necessary changes, and Move Forward! Apply the word of God to your situation, which is the Truth, and the Truth shall make you Free!

Declare: Something Great is going to happen for me today. Walk in Expectation.

<u>Action: What changes do you need to make?</u>

_____

_____

_____

_____

_____

_____

_____

_____

_____

_____

_____

_____

_____

_____

_____

_____

_____

_____

_____

Reflect

Things on my heart:

_____

_____

_____

_____

_____

_____

Things I'm grateful for:

_____

_____

_____

_____

_____

_____

Prayer Requests:

_____

_____

_____

_____

_____

_____

 *Declaration:*

I am free to love me!

Things on my heart...

Trust In Him

Proverbs 30:5 (KJV)

"Every word of God is pure: he is a shield
unto them that put their trust in him."

You may be going through some things and need God to make a way, heal your body, or open some doors in your favor. Just know that you can trust God and His Word. God will never leave you or forsake you. God has never failed you! His Promises are True.

Declare: Something Great is going to happen for me today.
Walk in Expectation.

Action: Write down your cares to God.

_____

_____

_____

_____

_____

_____

_____

_____

_____

_____

_____

_____

_____

_____

_____

_____

Reflect

Things on my heart:

_____
_____
_____
_____
_____
_____

Things I'm grateful for:

_____
_____
_____
_____
_____
_____

Prayer Requests:

_____
_____
_____
_____
_____
_____

 **Declaration:**

I am free to love me!

Things on my heart...

30-DAY SELF-CARE CHALLENGE

Check box once challenge is completed

☐ Set a personal goal for the month	☐ Practice deep breathing or meditation for 10 minutes	☐ Write a list of 10 things you're grateful for	☐ Take a walk outside	☐ Declutter a room or workspace
☐ Call or text a friend to catch up	☐ Cook a healthy meal	☐ Practice yoga or gentle stretching	☐ Write a positive affirmation and repeat it throughout the day	☐ Create a relaxing bedtime routine
☐ Journal about your thoughts and feelings	☐ Set aside time for your favorite hobby	☐ Give yourself a compliment	☐ Unplug from technology for an hour	☐ Listen to your favorite music or a calming playlist
☐ Practice mindfulness while doing everyday tasks	☐ Spend time with a pet or visit a local animal shelter	☐ Read a book or watch a movie that inspires you	☐ Explore a new relaxation method, like progressive muscle relaxation	☐ Take a power nap or restorative break
☐ Create a vision board or list of personal goals	☐ Volunteer or perform a random act of kindness	☐ Treat yourself to a small indulgence	☐ Reflect on your accomplishments and growth	☐ Connect with nature by visiting a park, beach, or forest
☐ Write a letter to your future self	☐ Set boundaries to protect your energy and time	☐ Establish a morning routine that energizes you	☐ Practice self-compassion and forgive yourself for past mistakes	☐ Review your progress and celebrate your achievements

God Will Supply All My Needs

Philippians 4:19 (KJV)

"But my God shall supply all your need according to his riches in glory by Christ Jesus."

free TO LOVE ME

Don't stress over not having enough to make ends meet. God will supply your need as He always does, and things will work out. You must Trust & Believe the Word of God. Keep the Faith.

Declare: Something Great is going to happen for me today. Walk in Expectation.

<u>Action: What do you need God to do for you?</u>

_____

_____

_____

_____

_____

_____

_____

_____

_____

_____

_____

_____

_____

_____

_____

_____

_____

_____

Reflect

Things on my heart:

_____

_____

_____

_____

_____

_____

Things I'm grateful for:

_____

_____

_____

_____

_____

_____

Prayer Requests:

_____

_____

_____

_____

_____

_____

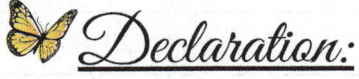 *Declaration:*

I am free to love me!

DATE:

Things on my heart...

Wait

Isaiah 40:31 (KJV)

"But they that wait upon the LORD shall renew their strength; they shall mount up with wings as eagles; they shall run, and not be weary; and they shall walk, and not faint."

free
TO LOVE ME

I encourage you to remain steadfast, trust in God's faithfulness, and have confidence that He will fulfill His promises in His perfect timing. Allow this time of waiting to grow spiritually, refine your character, and deepen your dependence on God. My prayer is that God will strengthen you during your wait. Wait on God. There is a blessing in your WAIT!

**Declare: Something Great is going to happen for me today.
Walk in Expectation.**

Action: What does the bible say about waiting?
Write four scriptures about waiting.

_____

_____

_____

_____

_____

_____

_____

_____

_____

_____

_____

_____

_____

_____

_____

_____

_____

_____

_____

Reflect

Things on my heart:

_____

_____

_____

_____

_____

_____

Things I'm grateful for:

_____

_____

_____

_____

_____

_____

Prayer Requests:

_____

_____

_____

_____

_____

_____

 ## Declaration:

I am free to love me!

Things on my heart...

Take Care Of You
1 Corinthians 6:19-20 (KJV)

"Do you not know that your body is a temple of the Holy Spirit who is within you, whom you have [received as a gift] from God and that you are not your own [property]? 20 You were bought with a price [you were actually purchased with the precious blood of Jesus and made His own]. So then, honor and glorify God with your body."

Learning to love and care for yourself is essential to enjoying and getting the most out of life. If you don't love and nurture who you are, it's impossible to maintain healthy and satisfying relationships with others. Don't allow past hurts, pain, resentment, and disappointments to keep you bitter, upset, unhappy, mean, angry, evil, and frustrated. Learn to Let it Go and Forgive. You Deserve a Fresh Beginning. You are Worthy of Love!

Declare: Something Great is going to happen for me today.
Walk in Expectation.
Action: What do you need to Let Go?

_____

_____

_____

_____

_____

_____

_____

_____

_____

_____

_____

_____

_____

_____

_____

_____

_____

_____

Reflect

Things on my heart:

_____
_____
_____
_____
_____
_____

Things I'm grateful for:

_____
_____
_____
_____
_____
_____

Prayer Requests:

_____
_____
_____
_____
_____
_____

 ## Declaration:

I am free to love me!

Things on my heart...

Make Your Request Known

Ephesians 3:20 (NLT)

"Now all glory to God, who is able, through his mighty power at work within us, to accomplish infinitely more than we might ask or think"

free
TO LOVE ME

Make your request known to God. Big or Small... God is waiting to hear from You. God can do More than you can Ask or Think! Nothing is Impossible with God!

Declare: Something Great is going to happen for me today. Walk in Expectation.

<u>Action: Write your requests below.</u>

_____

_____

_____

_____

_____

_____

_____

_____

_____

_____

_____

_____

_____

_____

_____

_____

_____

Reflect

Things on my heart:

_____
_____
_____
_____
_____
_____

Things I'm grateful for:

_____
_____
_____
_____
_____
_____

Prayer Requests:

_____
_____
_____
_____
_____

 **Declaration:**

I am free to love me!

Things on my heart...

Listen

Revelations 3:22 (NLT)

"Anyone with ears to hear must
listen to the Spirit and understand
what he is saying to the churches."

free
TO LOVE ME

You must learn to listen to the voice of God. What does God say about the decision you need to make, your healing, and your direction? Did you ask him?

Declare: Something Great is going to happen for me today.
Walk in Expectation.

Action: Take a few moments to ask Him below.

_____

_____

_____

_____

_____

_____

_____

_____

_____

_____

_____

_____

_____

_____

_____

_____

_____

Reflect

Things on my heart:

_____
_____
_____
_____
_____
_____

Things I'm grateful for:

_____
_____
_____
_____
_____
_____

Prayer Requests:

_____
_____
_____
_____
_____
_____

 *Declaration:*

I am free to love me!

Things on my heart...

Keep Your Eyes On God
Hebrews 12:2 (AMP)

"[looking away from all that will distract us and] focusing our eyes on Jesus, who is the Author and Perfecter of faith [the first incentive for our belief and the One who brings our faith to maturity], who for the joy [of accomplishing the goal] set before Him endured the cross, [a]disregarding the shame, and sat down at the right hand of the throne of God [revealing His deity, His authority, and the completion of His work]."

free
TO LOVE ME

Keep your eyes on God! Trust in Him and seek His kingdom and righteousness above all else. When you keep your mind and heart focused on God, you find strength, peace, and the assurance that He will provide for your needs. This reminds you to prioritize your relationship with God and seek His guidance and presence in all aspects of your life.

Declare: Something Great is going to happen for me today.
Walk in Expectation.

<u>Action: Write your thoughts.</u>

_____

_____

_____

_____

_____

_____

_____

_____

_____

_____

_____

_____

_____

_____

_____

_____

_____

_____

Reflect

Things on my heart:

_____
_____
_____
_____
_____
_____

Things I'm grateful for:

_____
_____
_____
_____
_____

Prayer Requests:

_____
_____
_____
_____
_____

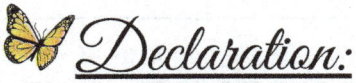

Declaration:

I am free to love me!

Things on my heart...

Forgive Yourself
Ephesians 4:31-32 (KJV)

"Let all bitterness and wrath, and anger, and clamor, and evil speaking be put away from you, with all malice: (32) Be ye kind one to another, tenderhearted, forgiving one another, even as God, for Christ's sake, hath forgiven you."

free
TO LOVE ME

Forgiving yourself and others can be difficult but necessary if you want the greatness God has in store for you! Forgiveness is not only about others but also about your spiritual growth and development. Love and unforgiveness cannot dwell in the same heart. If you choose to live out the love of God as the purpose for your life, then forgiving is an option that cannot be avoided.

Declare: Something Great is going to happen for me today.
Walk in Expectation.

<u>Action: What do you need to forgive yourself for?</u>

_____

_____

_____

_____

_____

_____

_____

_____

_____

_____

_____

_____

_____

_____

_____

_____

_____

_____

Reflect

Things on my heart:

_____
_____
_____
_____
_____
_____

Things I'm grateful for:

_____
_____
_____
_____
_____

Prayer Requests:

_____
_____
_____
_____
_____

 **Declaration:**

I am free to love me!

Things on my heart...

Press Toward The Mark
Philippians 3:13-14 (KJV)

"Brethren, I count not myself to have apprehended: but this one thing I do, forgetting those things which are behind, and reaching forth unto those things which are before, I press toward the mark for the prize of the high calling of God in Christ Jesus."

free
TO LOVE ME

Don't look at the past. Keep Pressing Forward! Keep praying and be patient. Things are going to work out for your good. God has a Plan and Purpose for your life.

Declare: Something Great is going to happen for me today. Walk in Expectation.

<u>Action: What area(s) do you need patience?</u>

_____

_____

_____

_____

_____

_____

_____

_____

_____

_____

_____

_____

_____

_____

_____

_____

_____

_____

_____

Reflect

Things on my heart:

_____

_____

_____

_____

_____

_____

Things I'm grateful for:

_____

_____

_____

_____

_____

Prayer Requests:

_____

_____

_____

_____

_____

 **Declaration:**

I am free to love me!

DATE:

Things on my heart...

Do Not Fear

Isaiah 41:10 (KJV)

"So do not fear, for I am with you; do not be dismayed, for I am your God. I will strengthen and help you and uphold you with my righteous right hand."

free
TO LOVE ME

God will work Everything out for your Good! Keep the Faith! Don't Give Up! God will work Everything out for your good. Fear cannot keep you shackled. Be courageous and break free from fear. In Jesus' Name Amen.

**Declare: Something Great is going to happen for me today.
Walk in Expectation.**

<u>Action: What do you Fear?</u>

_____

_____

_____

_____

_____

_____

_____

_____

_____

_____

_____

_____

_____

_____

_____

_____

_____

_____

_____

Reflect

Things on my heart:

_____
_____
_____
_____
_____
_____

Things I'm grateful for:

_____
_____
_____
_____
_____
_____

Prayer Requests:

_____
_____
_____
_____
_____
_____

 **Declaration:**

I am free to love me!

Things on my heart...

Strength and Dignity
Proverbs 31:25-26. (NLT)

"She is clothed with strength and dignity,
and she laughs without fear of the future.
When she speaks, her words are wise, and
she gives instructions with kindness."

free
TO LOVE ME

Laughter is like medicine. It's good for your Soul. It also confuses the devil when things are not how you want them to be. Just Laugh! EVERYTHING is working out for your Good!

Declare: Something Great is going to happen for me today. Walk in Expectation.

Action: Write ten kind words about yourself.

_____

_____

_____

_____

_____

_____

_____

_____

_____

_____

_____

_____

_____

_____

_____

_____

_____

_____

_____

Reflect

Things on my heart:

_____

_____

_____

_____

_____

_____

Things I'm grateful for:

_____

_____

_____

_____

_____

_____

Prayer Requests:

_____

_____

_____

_____

_____

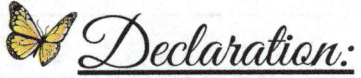 *Declaration:*

I am free to love me!

DATE:

Things on my heart...

GRATITUDE CHECK-IN

THE BEST THING THAT HAPPENED THIS WEEK

THINGS I LOVE ABOUT MYSELF

....
....
....
....
....
....
....
....
....

PEOPLE I'M GRATEFUL FOR

THINGS I LOOK FORWARD TO

THINGS THAT MAKE ME HAPPY

Small Beginnings
Job 8:7 (AMP)

"Though your beginning was insignificant,
Yet your end will significantly increase."

Don't focus on where you're at but look at how far you've come. Take one step at a time and watch your small beginnings expand into a greater horizon. You can Rejoice in advance about your future because God has some Great and Mighty things in store for You!

**Declare: Something Great is going to happen for me today.
Walk in Expectation.**

<u>Action:</u> Write down how far you've come, then celebrate yourself.

_____
_____
_____
_____
_____
_____
_____
_____
_____
_____
_____
_____
_____
_____
_____
_____
_____
_____

Reflect

Things on my heart:

_____
_____
_____
_____
_____
_____

Things I'm grateful for:

_____
_____
_____
_____
_____

Prayer Requests:

_____
_____
_____
_____
_____

 Declaration:

I am free to love me!

Things on my heart...

God Knows
Revelation 3:8 (AMP)

"I know your deeds. See, I have set before you an open door which no one can shut, for you have a little power, and have kept My word, and have not renounced or denied."

free
TO LOVE ME

God knows the work you are doing. No one can shut the door that God has opened for you. Keep trusting and believing what "God Said." Let your light shine bright for God.

**Declare: Something Great is going to happen for me today.
Walk in Expectation.**

<u>Action: What did God say?</u>

_____

_____

_____

_____

_____

_____

_____

_____

_____

_____

_____

_____

_____

_____

_____

_____

_____

Reflect

Things on my heart:

_____
_____
_____
_____
_____
_____

Things I'm grateful for:

_____
_____
_____
_____
_____
_____

Prayer Requests:

_____
_____
_____
_____
_____
_____

 Declaration:

I am free to love me!

Things on my heart...

Trust In The Lord
Proverbs 3:5-6 (AMP)

"Trust in and rely confidently on the Lord with all your heart, And do not rely on your own insight or understanding. n all your ways know and acknowledge and recognize Him, And He will make your paths straight and smooth [removing obstacles that block your way]."

free TO LOVE ME

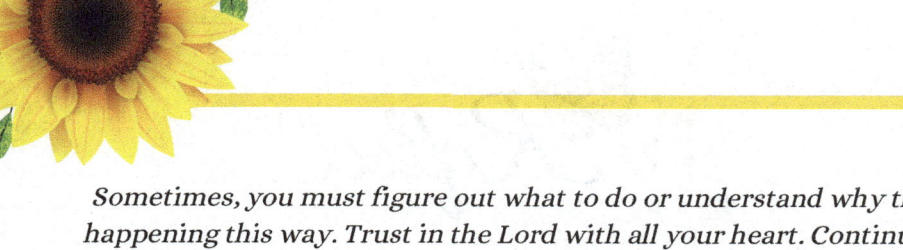

Sometimes, you must figure out what to do or understand why things are happening this way. Trust in the Lord with all your heart. Continue to Pray and do what God has instructed you to do. God has Everything under control!

Declare: Something Great is going to happen for me today.
Walk in Expectation.

Action: What has God instructed you to do?

_____

_____

_____

_____

_____

_____

_____

_____

_____

_____

_____

_____

_____

_____

_____

_____

_____

Reflect

Things on my heart:

_____

_____

_____

_____

_____

_____

Things I'm grateful for:

_____

_____

_____

_____

_____

_____

Prayer Requests:

_____

_____

_____

_____

_____

_____

 ## Declaration:

I am free to love me!

Things on my heart...

Laughter

Psalm 126:2 (AMP)

"Then our mouth was filled with laughter
And our tongue with joyful shouting;
Then they said among the nations, "The
Lord has done great things for them.""

free
TO LOVE ME

Sometimes you must laugh to keep from crying. Take this time to laugh and shout with joy. No matter what or how you feel. This, too, shall pass. The devil is a liar, defeated, has NO power over you, and can't stop or hinder God's plan for your life. Take back your joy. Take back your peace. Take control of your emotions. The blood of Jesus covers you. No weapon formed against you shall prosper! I speak life to every promise and dream. I command blessings to run you down and overtake you in Jesus' Name. Amen.

Declare: Something Great is going to happen for me today.
Walk in Expectation.

Action: What emotion do you need to take control of?

_____

_____

_____

_____

_____

_____

_____

_____

_____

_____

_____

_____

_____

_____

_____

_____

_____

_____

Reflect

Things on my heart:

_____
_____
_____
_____
_____
_____

Things I'm grateful for:

_____
_____
_____
_____
_____
_____

Prayer Requests:

_____
_____
_____
_____
_____
_____

 Declaration:

I am free to love me!

Things on my heart...

All About ME

These are a few of my favorite things:

Food:

Movie:

Book:

Animal:

Game:

Song:

Dessert:

Superhero:

Interesting Things About Me

Top Goal for this year

What makes me smile?

Show Love
Matthew 22:39 (AMP)

"The second is like it, 'You shall love your neighbor as yourself [that is, unselfishly seek the best or higher good for others]."

free
TO LOVE ME

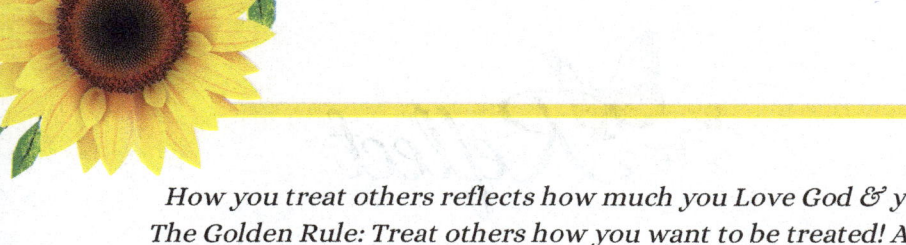

How you treat others reflects how much you Love God & yourself!
The Golden Rule: Treat others how you want to be treated! Allow this
to be your mindset, and then carry this out through your actions!

Declare: Something Great is going to happen for me today.
Walk in Expectation.

<u>Action: Write down ways you can show love to others.</u>

_____

_____

_____

_____

_____

_____

_____

_____

_____

_____

_____

_____

_____

_____

_____

_____

_____

_____

_____

Reflect

Things on my heart:

_____

_____

_____

_____

_____

_____

Things I'm grateful for:

_____

_____

_____

_____

_____

_____

Prayer Requests:

_____

_____

_____

_____

_____

_____

 Declaration:

I am free to love me!

DATE:

Things on my heart...

Words Have Power
Proverbs 18:21 (AMP)

"Death and life are in the power of the tongue, And those who love it and indulge it will eat its fruit and bear the consequences of their words."

free
TO LOVE ME

Your words possess the power to bring either life or death. The words you choose to speak can bring encouragement, healing, and life-giving affirmation, or they can cause harm, hurt, and destruction. You have a responsibility for what you say. You have a responsibility for what you say. You will reap the consequences or "eat the fruit" of your words.

**Declare: Something Great is going to happen for me today.
Walk in Expectation.**

<u>Action: Write positive words about your situation.</u>

_____

_____

_____

_____

_____

_____

_____

_____

_____

_____

_____

_____

_____

_____

_____

_____

_____

_____

_____

Reflect

Things on my heart:

_____
_____
_____
_____
_____
_____

Things I'm grateful for:

_____
_____
_____
_____
_____

Prayer Requests:

_____
_____
_____
_____

 Declaration:

I am free to love me!

DATE:

Things on my heart...

_____

_____

_____

_____

_____

_____

_____

_____

_____

_____

_____

_____

_____

_____

_____

_____

_____

_____

_____

_____

_____

_____

Pure Heart

Psalm 51:10 (KJV)

"Create in me a clean heart, O God, and renew a right spirit within me."

free

TO LOVE ME

Mediate daily on the word of God. Your heart must be pure because it can hinder your Blessings. Don't hold on to bitterness, anger, unforgiveness, discord, and grudges. Let Go and Let God!

**Declare: Something Great is going to happen for me today.
Walk in Expectation.**

Action: Do a heart check-up. Write down your assessment.

_____

_____

_____

_____

_____

_____

_____

_____

_____

_____

_____

_____

_____

_____

_____

_____

_____

_____

Reflect

Things on my heart:

_____

_____

_____

_____

_____

_____

Things I'm grateful for:

_____

_____

_____

_____

_____

_____

Prayer Requests:

_____

_____

_____

_____

_____

 **Declaration:**

I am free to love me!

Things on my heart...

Grace
1 Samuel 16:7 (KJV)

"But the Lord said to Samuel, "Do not look on his appearance or on the height of his stature, because I have rejected him. For the Lord sees not as man sees: man looks on the outward appearance, but the Lord looks on the heart."

free
TO LOVE ME

This is one example of how God has extended Grace to us by looking beyond our faults and seeing our needs – our need for a Savior, our need for forgiveness, our need for love, and our need for Him.

Declare: Something Great is going to happen for me today.
Walk in Expectation.

<u>Action: To whom do you need to extend Grace?</u>

_____

_____

_____

_____

_____

_____

_____

_____

_____

_____

_____

_____

_____

_____

_____

_____

_____

_____

Reflect

Things on my heart:

_____

_____

_____

_____

_____

_____

Things I'm grateful for:

_____

_____

_____

_____

_____

Prayer Requests:

_____

_____

_____

_____

_____

 **Declaration:**

I am free to love me!

Things on my heart...

Jafora Fox is a remarkable individual driven by a divine purpose to empower and uplift others on their journey toward greatness. With unwavering faith in God and an unyielding passion for helping people fulfill their God-given assignments, she has dedicated her life to making a positive difference in the lives of others.

As the CEO of Jafora Fox Inc., Jafora offers her transformative services as a highly sought-after Transformational & Leadership Coach and Speaker. Her expertise and guidance have helped countless individuals unlock their full potential and achieve remarkable personal and professional growth.

Jafora's commitment to spreading her message of empowerment extends beyond her coaching services. As the host of the renowned Jafora Fox Show: Let's Talk Business & Renew Your Mind, she shares her wisdom and insights with a broad audience through engaging weekly live streams on Facebook, LinkedIn, and YouTube. Her show has become a trusted source of inspiration and guidance for those seeking to excel in their personal and business endeavors.

In addition to her entrepreneurial pursuits, Jafora Fox is the visionary Founder of "Free to Love Me," an organization dedicated to providing transformative coaching and development programs for women and girls. Through workshops focused on self-esteem, character building, anger management, and conflict resolution, she empowers individuals to overcome obstacles and embrace their true potential.

Jafora Fox is an ardent advocate of lifelong learning and academic excellence. She is pursuing a Ph.D. in Business Administration specializing in Industrial/Organizational Psychology from National University. Driven by her love for education, she obtained a master's degree in counseling from Seton Hall University, an MBA with a concentration in Management from Keller Graduate School of Management, and a bachelor's degree in psychology from Spelman College.

Beyond her professional achievements, Jafora finds immense joy in her personal life. She is married to the love of her life, Deacon Derrick Fox. They share four wonderful children, a beautiful daughter in love, and five adorable grandsons. Jafora cherishes the blessings of love, unity, and support that her family brings.

Jafora Fox believes that challenges are not roadblocks but growth opportunities. Through her steadfast commitment to helping others and relentless pursuit of personal and professional excellence, she inspires individuals worldwide to overcome challenges and embrace a life filled with purpose and fulfillment.

Connect with me...

Website: www.jaforafox.com
Email: info@jaforafox.com

FB: Jafora Fox Inc
IG: Jafora Fox Inc
LinkedIn Profile: Jafora Fox Inc

Made in the USA
Coppell, TX
15 November 2024